Wool
Embroidery
and Design

Wool Embroidery and Design

LEE LOCKHEED

NEW
HOLLAND

Publisher's Note

As readers from Australia, the United Kingdom and the United States of America will be using this book, the materials that may not be readily available in all countries have been listed below together with suggested alternatives.

Wool Blanketing

This is a 100% wool fabric used in the manufacture of bed blankets. Ready-made items such as baby blankets with bound edges may be used instead. A ready-made blanket, cut to size to suit the relevant project, would make a good substitute while fairly loosely woven thick wool fabric should also give acceptable results.

Beading Lace

This is a lace that incorporates eyelet edging, either with or without ribbon threaded through the eyelet holes. If ribbon has not been supplied you can insert your own ribbon in a colour of your choice. Edging lace of any type can be used instead.

Silk Ribbon

Silk Ribbon is soft and flexible and is as easy to work with as tapestry wool. If not available, use fine embroidery ribbon or very thin satin ribbon but this will not lie as effectively. Another option would be to use an entirely different thread, such as stranded cotton.

Marlitt Thread

This is used for its glossy appearance, so the best alternative would be any 100% polyester or cotton/polyester stranded thread.

First published in the UK in 1992 by
New Holland (Publishers) Ltd
37 Connaught Street, London W2 2AZ

Copyright © 1992 Lee Lockheed

ISBN 1 85368 219 5

Editors: Tracy Marsh, Debi McCulloch

Designer: Kel Gibb

Photographer: Adam Bruzzone

Phototypeset and origination by Image Color, Adelaide, South Australia

Printed and bound in Hong Kong by Dai Nippon Printing Co

Dedication

This book is dedicated to Mrs. Eunice ('Nougie') Manouge, my friend, mentor and gifted craftswoman, who through her encouragement inspired me to appreciate my own natural talent.

Acknowledgements

I would like to thank my husband, Richard, and my two daughters, Sarah and Amy, for their patience, tolerance, love and assistance they have given me during the time that I have been, not only writing, but also creating the projects and preparing the illustrations that have been used in the book.

In addition, I would like to thank Richard for the many hours spent carefully transcribing my handwritten manuscript into the typed word, as well as drawing the technical diagrams on pages 18, 23 and 24.

To the following individuals and companies I would like to offer my sincere thanks for their encouragement and assistance:

Deborah Bohanes, for her constructive criticism, support and encouragement.

My many students who have so freely and consistently given me incentive and reassurance to produce this book.

Onkaparinga Woollen Company, Lobethal, South Australia.

XLN Fabrics, for the fabrics on the Child's Dressing Gown Set.

Kismet Gallery, Adelaide, for the muslin used in the Pot Pourri Bag.

Valerie Kidd, Jane Smith and Chris Oswald, for the loan of items used for photography.

Anna Thurlow, for modelling the Child's Dressing Gown Set.

Eunice Manouge, for knitting the baby's white cardigan.

Shauna Thorn, for allowing me to embroider her white jumper.

Jess Burton, for knitting the baby's pink cardigan.

Glenys James, for knitting the baby's booties.

Contents

Introduction

Flowers have always been a source of wonderment and inspiration for us all. Artists from all disciplines throughout the ages have striven to capture the enchanting beauty of floral designs. As the painter uses oils to emulate nature's image, the embroiderer expresses one's self through the diligent and selective use of a myriad of wools and threads of widely varying textures and hues. Wool is an excellent medium in which to work as it enables the novice to create simple but satisfying designs. It also allows the more experienced and daring embroiderers to experiment with the endless possibilities available, enabling them to create their own unique masterpieces. My aim in writing this book is to provide the inspiration and background technical knowledge to pick up a needle and create.

Materials

THREADS

For the projects featured in this book, the following wools and threads have been chosen, all readily available through most specialist embroidery outlets:

- DMC Tapestry Wools (Art No. 486), lightly twisted 4 ply.

- DMC Broder Medicis (Art No. 475), 2 ply Crewel Wool.

- DMC Perlé Cotton (Art No. 115), twisted thread with a light sheen, made in different thicknesses. The higher the number the finer the thread.

- DMC Stranded Cotton (Art No. 117), 100% cotton lustrous thread in six separable strands.

- Appleton's Crewel Wool, fine 2 ply wool.

- Marlitt, a polyester thread with a shiny finish, in four separable strands.

- Silk Ribbon, 100% silk.

- Metallic Thread, available in varying qualities; only some are washable.

The heavy texture of DMC tapestry wool adds a wonderful dimension to larger flowers such as roses and daisies. The Appleton's, Medicis, Marlitt and silk ribbons, on the other hand, are more subtle and finely textured, which gives the embroidery a delicate feminine look.
When embroidering, do not use too long a thread; 50 cm (20 ins) is quite sufficient. If the thread wears thin or fluffs up, replace it immediately.

FABRICS

- 100% wool blanketing.

- Any fabric which will allow the thread to pass through with a minimum of stress on the thread is suitable. Wool embroidery can be used to embellish almost any fabric.

NEEDLES

Needles vary in thickness, length, size of eye and sharpness of point. A number indicates the size; the higher the number, the finer the needle.

- DMC Tapestry Wool—Size 18 Tapestry

- Appleton's Crewel Wool ⎤
  DMC Perlé Cotton
  DMC Stranded Cotton   Size 5/10
  DMC Broder Medicis   Embroidery Crewel
  Marlitt Thread
  Metallic Thread ⎦

- Silk Ribbon—Size 24 or 26 Chenille or Tapestry

SCISSORS

A high quality pair of embroidery scissors is essential. The scissors should be small and sharp with pointed blades and perfectly closing points.

THIMBLE

You may prefer to work without a thimble, however, it is useful for protecting the middle finger when pushing the needle through the fabric. Buy a good quality one and make sure it fits well. A silver or leather thimble can prove to be a good investment.

EMBROIDERY FRAME OR HOOP

The use of an embroidery frame or hoop is a personal choice. An embroidery hoop was used only for the two cushion cover projects.

Transferring Designs

Unfortunately, when working with wool blanket, because of its texture, there are no easy ways of transferring the designs. The method found to be most successful is to trace the design onto good quality tracing paper. Tack or pin the design onto the blanket and with a sharp lead pencil or a water soluble fabric pen, pierce a hole through the centre of each flower on the tracing paper, making sure to mark a small dot on the fabric. When you remove the tracing paper you are left with the dots that locate the centre of each flower on which you can now work the design. If embroidering a large design break it up into smaller and more workable sections.

TRANSFERRING BOWS
To transfer the bow, cut out the template of paper and tack to the blanket. Using the same colour thread as for the bow, tack the shape of the bow onto the blanket. Unpick the tacking on the template and remove it. Satin stitch the bow, working either side of the tacking stitches.

For transferring designs onto fabrics that have a smooth texture, such as cottons and linens, use dressmaker's tracing paper.

Colour and Design

To a talented few, putting together a successful colour scheme is easy, but for most people, the idea of choosing their colour scheme and design can be totally daunting.

The ideal way when designing your colour schemes is to borrow ideas from Mother Nature, artists and books. Need inspiration? Look no further than your garden. You will find that it contains a comprehensive source of ideas and reveals subtlety and surprise. Spend some time to look at the detail and more ideas for colour, shape and patterns will become evident. Take the pink of a rose, notice the variation between a new bud and the flower in full bloom and appreciate the varying shades of purple and mauves in lavender and wisteria. Daisies provide us with vivid whites, sky blues and sunny yellows, whilst a bed of nasturtiums contains deep yellows, oranges, reds and lemons. Observe closely the green in your garden. The leaves and foliage contain a wide range of green–grey green, blue green, lime green, bottle green, silver grey and many more. A thread basket should contain more shades of green than any other colour.

Take a stroll along the beach and look at the colours of seashells. You will find colours of beige, off white, honey, deep browns, smoky blues, silver greys, some blended with the softest pinks, mauves and oranges.

Ethnic colour schemes provide us with a multitude of vibrant and unusual colour combinations, such as chilli reds, saffron, brilliant purples, emerald green, mango and hot pinks.

When designing your work it is not necessary to use masses of stitches. A few well chosen ones, varying the size and texture, will provide you with exciting results. Emphasize a certain feature and play down the surrounding flowers and foliage. A perfect example of this is the dominance of the daisies worked on the blanket, 'Springtime', on page 29.

Fabrics, too, can also play an important part in stimulating your creativity when utilizing colour. A patterned fabric which contains a mixture of colours, such as Liberty Print or a pretty floral, can provide you with the basis for an embroidery scheme, simply by extracting each individual colour from within the print. An excellent example of extracting colour from a print is shown on the 'Child's Dressing Gown Set' on page 41. In this case, the fabric, a striped border print, was the total inspiration, not only for the choice of colour, but also for the embroidery pattern itself.

Become aware of your environment. We are surrounded by visual sources of colour and inspiration.

Blankets

The Victorian era is lovingly remembered for its obsessive passion for ornate and beautiful decorative work of all kinds. It is from this era that the art of wool embroidery evolved. Conjure up nostalgic images from those days long gone by embroidering charming blankets like Grandma's Knee Rug, Springtime and Baby's Blanket.

Grandma's Knee Rug

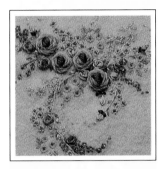

Everyone loves a present that is personalised. Delight a very special Grandma by presenting her with a gift, straight from the heart, which will take her back to the days of her own childhood.

MATERIALS:

Woollen blanket piece (pink)—length 112 cm (44 ins), width 76 cm (30 ins).

4 metres (4^1/$_3$ yds) of beading lace.

5 metres (5^1/$_2$ yds) of cotton lace—width 5 cm (2 ins).

5 metres (5^1/$_2$ yds) of double sided satin ribbon.

DMC Tapestry Wools—7226 (deep pink), 7223 (lighter shade of pink), 7221 (lightest shade of pink).

Appleton's Crewel Wools—141 (pale pink), 692 (yellow), 292 (deep green), 352 (pale green), 712 (pink).

DMC Broder Medicis—8405 (green), 113 (pink).

Marlitt Thread—1213 (pink).

Silk Ribbon—21 (green), 163 (pink).

PROCEDURE:

1. The heart template pattern (page 19) is half size. To enlarge the pattern to its actual size use either of the following two methods.

(a) Trace the heart pattern onto a sheet of paper and construct a grid of squares 2 x 2 cm (^{3}/$_4$ x ^{3}/$_4$ in) to cover the pattern. Construct another grid of the same number of squares, but this time each square being 4 x 4 cm (1^1/$_2$ x 1^1/$_2$ ins). Carefully copy the design of the heart square by square onto the larger grid.

(b) Enlarge the pattern on a photocopier by firstly increasing the original by 141% and then enlarge the new image also by 141%. If you are lucky enough to have access to a photocopier with a 200% enlargement factor, this will give the correct size instantly.

2. To transfer the heart pattern to the rug, cut out a thin cardboard template and pin it in the centre of the rug. Embroider a stem stitch around the heart using the deep green Appleton's number 292 fine Crewel wool.

3. Refer to the heart embroidery design (page 21) for a placement guide for the embroidered flowers, leaves and stems. For detailed information on transferring the design to your rug refer to page 12. This design is also half size.

4. The design for the corner spray (page 20) is actual size and is worked on three corners, omitting the top right hand corner where you will place your bow, if using the lace finish.

FINISH:

1. To prepare your blanket for attaching the lace edging, use one of the following methods:

(a) Overlock the edge of your blanket using an overlocker.

(b) Set your sewing machine on your widest zigzag stitch. For example, a stitch length of four and a width of four. It would be beneficial to experiment with your own machine on a small piece of blanket until you achieve the effect that you desire.

(c) Blanket stitch by hand.

2.   Commence attaching the lace at the top left hand corner of the blanket. Allow 5 cm (2 ins) of lace to overlap the corner as shown at A on diagram 1.

3.   Slightly gather your lace as you slip stitch it to your blanket. Stop gathering your lace 9 cm (3$^1/_2$ ins) from the corner (point B).

4.   Work all four sides of the blanket, ensuring to gather the lace 9 cm (3$^1/_2$ ins) both sides of the corners.

5.   When you have completed all four sides of the blanket, turn the overlapping lace under on a 45 degree angle. Tack into place, cut off excess lace and overstitch by hand.

6.   Slip stitch your beading lace to hold it firmly in place on your blanket. Thread the ribbon through and tie a bow at the top right hand corner.

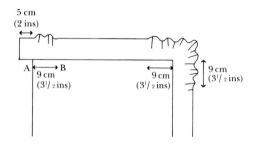

Diagram 1 (not to scale)

Heart template pattern (half size)

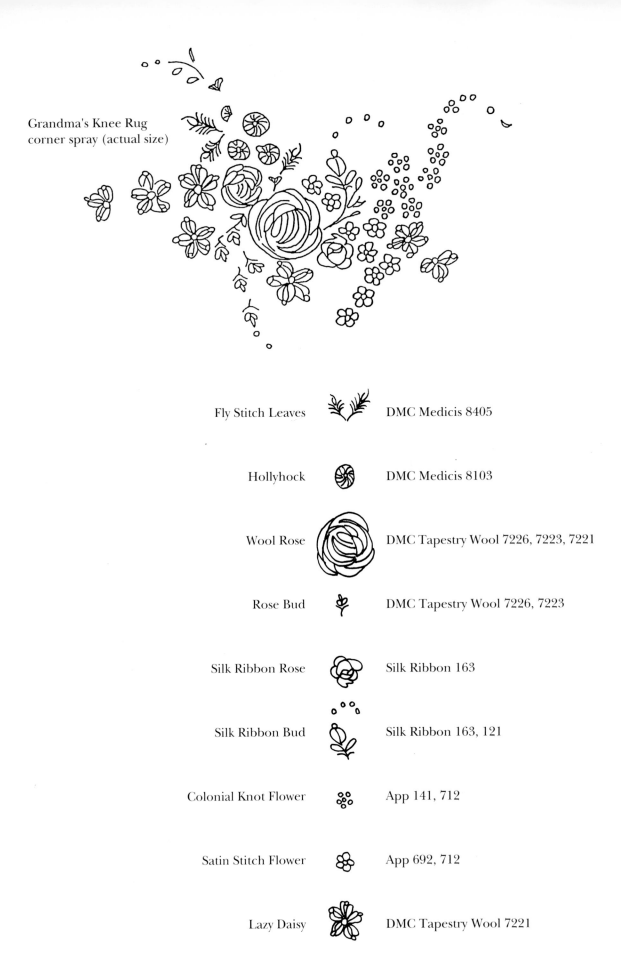

Grandma's Knee Rug
corner spray (actual size)

Fly Stitch Leaves		DMC Medicis 8405
Hollyhock		DMC Medicis 8103
Wool Rose		DMC Tapestry Wool 7226, 7223, 7221
Rose Bud		DMC Tapestry Wool 7226, 7223
Silk Ribbon Rose		Silk Ribbon 163
Silk Ribbon Bud		Silk Ribbon 163, 121
Colonial Knot Flower		App 141, 712
Satin Stitch Flower		App 692, 712
Lazy Daisy		DMC Tapestry Wool 7221

Grandma's Knee Rug (half size)

Amy's Cot Blanket

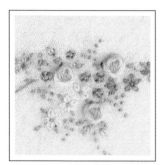

Sugar and spice and all things nice—that's what little girls are made of. Pamper that special little baby girl with her own childhood treasure. Embroider a soft cuddly blanket with her initials surrounded by four sprays of delicate flowers worked in the softest of colours.

MATERIALS:
Cream blanket piece length 90 cm (36 ins), width 63 cm (25 ins).
3.2 metres (3½ yds) of cotton lace width 2 cm (¾ in).
3.2 metres (3½ yds) of double sided satin blanket binding (cream).
DMC Tapestry Wools—7215 (deep apricot), 7192 (lighter shade of apricot), 7191 (pale apricot).
Appleton's Crewel Wools—692 (yellow), 741 (blue), 707 (apricot), 353 (green).

PROCEDURE:
1.   To obtain an embroidery design of the actual size used in this project, enlarge the design (page 25) on a photocopier set on 141%. The design for the corner spray (page 25) is actual size.
2.   To transfer the design to your blanket, refer to 'Transferring Designs' on page 12.
3.   For this rug, the DMC Tapestry Wool has been split in half. If you wish to split the wool in this way, use strands no longer than 30 cm (12 ins) as the wool tends to disintegrate.

FINISH:
1.   Lay the blanket flat with the embroidered side facing upwards. Place the satin binding underneath the left hand side to the blanket allowing 3.5 cm (1½ ins) of binding to overlap above the corner (diagram 1).
2.   Fold the top edge of the binding (AB) back over the blanket (diagram 2).

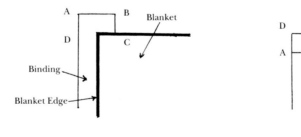

Diagram 1   Diagram 2

3.   Fold the top left hand corner of the binding (point D) diagonally across to the edge of the blanket (diagram 3).
4.   Fold the binding over the blanket, forming a neat 45 degree diagonal cornerpiece and then tack into place (diagram 4).

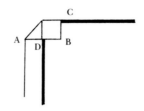

Diagram 3

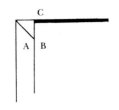

Diagram 4

5. Carefully position the binding and commence tacking around the blanket. At the three remaining corners, fold the binding under to form a 45 degree diagonal, neatly position and tack into place.

6. When reaching the top left hand corner of the blanket, cut off the excess binding leaving 3.5 cm (1¹/₂ ins) overlap (diagram 5). Fold the overlap into an arrowhead (diagrams 6a, b, c).

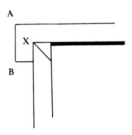

Diagram 5

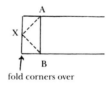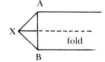

fold corners over

Diagram 6a   Diagram 6b   Diagram 6c

7. Fold the satin binding over the top edge of the blanket forming a diagonal cornerpiece, which can then be neatly positioned adjacent to the diagonal piece constructed previously and then tack into place (diagram 7).

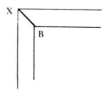

Diagram 7

8. Handsew with fine slip stitch, working both the front and back of the corner.

9. Zigzag your binding to the blanket using your widest zigzag stitch on your sewing machine. An Elna machine set at width 4 and length 4 was used. Unpick your tacking stitches.

10. Slip stitch the lace immediately below the binding, gathering it slightly at all four corners.

11. Using the Appleton's apricot (707), stem stitch around the edge of the lace.

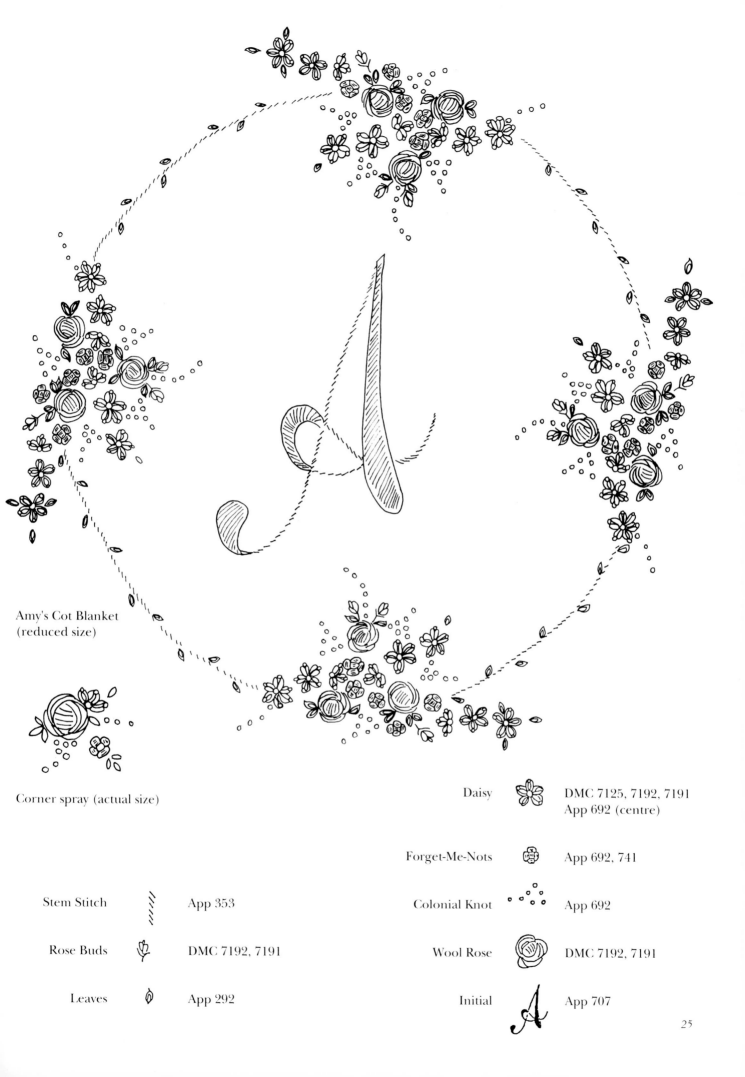

Amy's Cot Blanket
(reduced size)

Corner spray (actual size)

Stem Stitch		App 353
Rose Buds		DMC 7192, 7191
Leaves		App 292

Daisy		DMC 7125, 7192, 7191 App 692 (centre)
Forget-Me-Nots		App 692, 741
Colonial Knot		App 692
Wool Rose		DMC 7192, 7191
Initial		App 707

N O P Q
R S T
U V W
X Y Z

Springtime

Flowers have always been a source of inspiration and wonderment for us all and at what better time of the year than during the early days of springtime can we fully appreciate the magnificent splendour of a garden bursting into bloom beneath a brilliant clear sky.

This delightful garland of springtime flowers has been created by the effective use of simple stitchery and the careful blending of heavy and fine thread. Marlitt has also been used to form dew-like effects on the smaller flowers.

MATERIALS:

Woollen blanket piece (sky blue)—length 75 cm (30 ins), width 54 cm (22 ins).

3 metres (3¹/₃ yds) of cotton lace—width 5 cm (2 ins).

3.2 metres (3¹/₂ yds) of ribbon (pink).

2.7 metres (3 yds) of beading lace.

Marlitt Thread—895 (green), 1207 (pink), 1042 (apricot), 1036 (cream), 1059 (blue).

Appleton's Crewel Wools—692 (yellow), 741 (blue), 744 (blue), 886 (blue), 876 (light blue), 706 (apricot), 707 (apricot), 753 (pink), 881 (cream), 641 (green), 642 (green), 342 (green), 292 (green).

DMC Broder Medicis—8119 (pink), 8223 (pink), 8225 (pink), 8221 (blue).

DMC Stranded Cotton—Ecru.

PROCEDURE:

1. To obtain an embroidery design of the actual size used in this project, enlarge Springtime design (page 31) on a photocopier set on 141%.

2. Transfer the design to the middle of your blanket piece. Refer to 'Transferring Designs' on page 12 for more detailed information.

3. When using Marlitt thread, work a colonial knot with your wool. Bring your needle threaded with a single strand of Marlitt up through the centre of the wool knot. Work a second colonial knot with the Marlitt, nestling it into the centre of the original wool knot.

FINISH:

1. This blanket has been finished with a lace edging as used with 'Grandma's Knee Rug' and for information on completing your blanket in this way, refer to page 17.

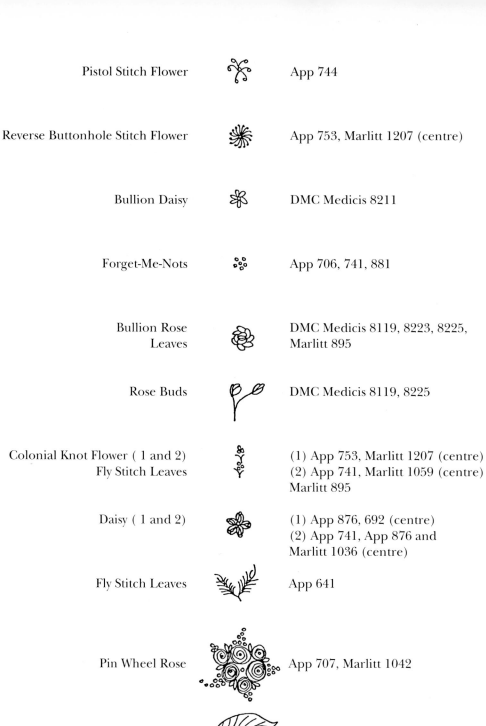

Pistol Stitch Flower — App 744

Reverse Buttonhole Stitch Flower — App 753, Marlitt 1207 (centre)

Bullion Daisy — DMC Medicis 8211

Forget-Me-Nots — App 706, 741, 881

Bullion Rose
Leaves — DMC Medicis 8119, 8223, 8225,
Marlitt 895

Rose Buds — DMC Medicis 8119, 8225

Colonial Knot Flower (1 and 2)
Fly Stitch Leaves — (1) App 753, Marlitt 1207 (centre)
(2) App 741, Marlitt 1059 (centre)
Marlitt 895

Daisy (1 and 2) — (1) App 876, 692 (centre)
(2) App 741, App 876 and
Marlitt 1036 (centre)

Fly Stitch Leaves — App 641

Pin Wheel Rose — App 707, Marlitt 1042

Satin Stitch leaf — App 342

Half Daisy — DMC Stranded Cotton Ecru, App 692

Daisy — DMC Stranded Cotton Ecru, App 692

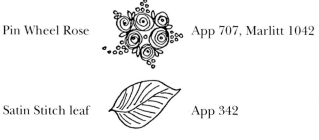

Bow — App 886

Springtime (reduced Size)

Simply Irresistible

This delightful little rug is simplicity itself with universal appeal. For the novice embroiderer this project is an excellent introduction to working with wool.

MATERIALS:

Pure woollen blanket piece (cream)—length 110 cm (44 ins), width 74 cm (30 ins).
4.2 metres (4²/₃ yds) of cotton lace—width 5 cm (2 ins).
4 metres (4¹/₃ yds) of cotton lace beading.
4.2 metres (4²/₃ yds) of double sided satin ribbon.
DMC Tapestry Wools—7215 (apricot), 7192 (apricot), 7191 (apricot), 7302 (blue), white.
Appleton's Crewel Wools—692 (yellow), 351 (green), 292 (green).
DMC Broder Medicis—8211 (pale blue).
2.5 metres (2³/₄ yds) of silk ribbon (cream).

PROCEDURE:

1. Construct a circle with a diameter of approximately 36 cm (14 ins) in the centre of the blanket. (A useful hint is to use a large dinner plate to make a circle template.) Pin the template to your blanket and tack around it using one of your Appleton's green wools.
2. To obtain four evenly spaced points on the circumference of the circle, fold the template in half and tack a diameter across the circle. Rotate the template 90 degrees and tack another diameter lengthwise across the circle.
3. The embroidery design for Simply Irresistible (page 35) is used on each quadrant of the circle. The corner spray design is embroidered on three corners of the blanket omitting the corner where you have tied your bow. For information on transferring your design to your blanket, refer to 'Transferring Designs' on page 12.

FINISH:

1. This blanket has been finished with a lace edging as used with 'Grandma's Knee Rug' and for information on completing your blanket, refer to page 17.

| Forget Me Nots | | DMC Tapestry Wool 7302,
App 692 (centre) |

Forget Me Nots DMC Tapestry Wool 7302,
App 692 (centre)

Stem and Leaves App 351, 292

Rose Bud
Leaves DMC Tapestry Wool 7192, 7191
App 351

Hollyhock DMC Medicis 8211

Pistol Stitch Flower App 692

Silk Ribbon Rose Cream Silk ribbon

Daisy DMC Tapestry Wool white
App 692 (centre)

Wool Rose DMC Tapestry Wool 7215, 7192, 7191

Simply Irresistible (actual size)

Corner spray (actual size)

Baby's Blanket

The symbol of love and friendship, the heart, is used to its optimum here. Add a new dimension to your work by combining wool embroidery, applique and the creative use of gold thread onto a blanket of red. This delightful design could also be used to decorate the front of a child's windcheater or jumper.

MATERIALS:
Woollen blanket piece (red)—length and width, 60 cm (24 ins).
2.7 metres (3 yds) of red satin blanket binding.
Small piece of white felt.
Polyester filling.
Appleton's Crewel Wools—692 (yellow), 876 and 741 (blues), 501 and 503 (reds), 751 and 753 (pinks), 602, 932 (mauves), 351 and 352 (greens), white.
Dewhurst Gold Thread,—2144D.

PROCEDURE:
1.   Cut out a heart and bow template using the embroidery design (page 39) and tack it to your blanket. Refer to 'Transferring Designs' on page 12 for more information.
2.   Satin stitch the bow.
3.   Threading your needle with the Appleton's fine wool and the gold thread, stem stitch around both sides of the heart.
4.   Tack the felt ducks to the blanket leaving a small opening in which to insert the polyester filling.
5.   After padding the ducks with polyester filling, stem stitch around the edge of the ducks using the Appleton's white wool.

FINISH:
1.   This blanket has a satin binding finish as used on 'Amy's Cot Blanket'. For more information refer to page 23.

Lazy Daisy Leaves App 351, 352

Roses Blue—App 876, 741
Mauve—App 602, 932
Pink—App 751, 753
Red—App 501, 503

Fly Stitch Leaves App 352

Lazy Daisy Flowers Pink—App 751
Blue—App 741
Mauve—App 602

Ducks White Felt

Stem Stitch
Herringbone Stitch App 692
Gold Thread 2144D

Half Bow App 692
Gold Thread 2144D

Full Bow App 692
Gold Thread 2144D

Baby's Blanket (actual size)

Child's Dressing Gown Set

Cold dark nights, log fires, small children bathed and dressed warmly for bed. Create this idyllic scene by embroidering a gift of love fit for a princess. Fabric of soft mauve and white stripes, tiny pink spots and a border of roses was the inspiration for this delightful little girl's dressing gown set.

Dressing Gown, Coathanger and Pot Pourri Bag

Dressing Gown

A child's lined coat pattern, which included a hood, was used to create an extra warm and cuddly effect to this traditional style gown.

MATERIALS:

Select a pattern of your own choice.

Pure wool blanketing (see pattern for quantity).

Cotton border print fabric (see pattern for quantity).

Button covering kit—size 19 mm ($^3/_4$ in).

2 metres ($2^1/_4$ yds) of satin binding.

Appleton's Crewel Wools—754 (pink), 752 (pale pink), 932 (purple), 602 (pale purple), 692 (yellow), 154 (green), 641 (pale green).

PROCEDURE:

1.   To transfer the embroidery design (below) onto the pocket piece, refer to 'Transferring Designs' on page 12.

2.   Embroider the pocket piece using the key on page 48. Line it with the lining fabric and edge with the satin binding.

3.   Iron a piece of satin binding flat and embroider with tiny leaves and roses. Make into buttons using the button kit.

4.   Construct the gown according to the pattern instructions, adding satin binding to the hood and sleeve edges.

FINISH:

1.   For an extra finish, stem stitch around the edge of the satin binding using Appleton's 754 (pink).

Dressing Gown Pocket (actual size)

Coathanger

The child's coathanger contains no padding and can be easily slipped off to launder.

MATERIALS:
1 small wooden coathanger.
20 cm (8 ins) of fabric.
1 metre (39 ins) of 7 mm ($^1/_4$ in) ribbon.
Small piece of organdie fabric.
Rose pot pourri.
Marlitt Thread—1019 (pink).

PROCEDURE:
1.   Cut a double piece of fabric, 35.5 x 10 cm (14 x 4 ins) to fit the shape of the hanger.
2.   Make up the coathanger cover by stitching a seam down both short ends and across the top. Leave 2.5 cm (1 in) open in the middle for the hook. Fold right side out.
3.   Cut a fabric strip 1.2 metres x 7.5 cm (47 x 3 ins) for the bottom frill. Gather to fit the bottom of the coathanger cover.
4.   Sew the frill around the bottom.
5.   Slip the cover over the coathanger with the hook protruding through the opening on the top edge.
6.   Cover the hanger hook with the satin ribbon, leaving enough ribbon at the base of the hook to tie a bow around the pot pourri bag.
7.   For an extra finish, stem stitch around the seams and along the top of the frill using Marlitt 1019 (pink).

Pot Pourri Bag

A tiny bag made of fine organdie and filled with sweet smelling rose pot pourri adds a special finishing touch to the coathanger.

1.   Cut a piece of organdie 40 x 14 cm ($15^3/_4$ x $5^1/_2$ ins).
2.   Fold the bag in half and sew up the side seams, turn right side out. Fold over 6 cm ($2^1/_2$ ins) at the top.
3.   Half fill the bag with rose pot pourri.
4.   Gather around the bag by hand 3.5 cm ($1^1/_2$ ins) from the top. Pull the gathering threads tight and anchor off.
5.   Tie the bag to the coathanger with the leftover ribbon at the base of the hook.

Slippers

The pattern provided for the slippers is a size three. For other sizes, cut a sole to fit the child's foot and shorten or lengthen the back seam of the pattern piece provided.

MATERIALS:
Piece of soft leather.
Piece of blanketing.
1.2 metres (47 ins) of satin binding.
1.4 metres (55 ins) of 15 mm ($^5/_8$ in) of satin ribbon.
Quick drying craft glue.
Appleton's Crewel Wools—754 (pink), 752 (pale pink), 932 (purple), 602 (light purple), 692 (yellow), 154 (green), 641 (pale green).

PROCEDURE:
1.   Cut two shoe soles of leather and two of lining using the Slippers pattern (page 49).
2.   Cut two shoe uppers of blanket and two of lining.
3.   Cut two pieces of satin binding, 5 cm (2 ins) in length.
4.   Transfer the Slippers design (page 48) onto the two pieces of blanket. Refer to 'Transferring Designs' on page 12.
5.   Embroider the design onto blanket uppers.
6.   Apply a thin line of glue around the edge of the leather soles, shiny side up and stick the fabric lining to the soles, right sides facing up.
7.   Stitch a 5 mm ($^1/_4$ in) back seam on the lining and blanket uppers.
8.   Fold the 5 cm (2 ins) of satin binding in half and tack in place, open ends facing up, onto the centre back of the blanket uppers, forming a loop for the ribbon to pass through.
9.   Tack the top of the lining and blanket uppers together, right sides facing in and sew a 5 mm ($^1/_4$ in) seam.
10. Turn right sides out, press and tack the lining and blanket together around the bottom of the uppers.
11. With right sides facing up, sew uppers to the soles.
12. Machine sew the satin binding around the edge of the leather sole, placing the join at the centre back.
13. Fold binding over and hand stitch in place on the blanket uppers.

FINISH:
1.   Using the Appleton's 754 (pink), stem stitch around the edge of the satin binding and the top of the uppers.
2.   Thread the ribbon through the back loop and tie a bow around the ankle.

Slippers and Hot Water Bottle Cover

Hot Water Bottle Cover

Small clusters of roses and daisies, adapted from the border print design, decorate the Hot Water Bottle Cover.

MATERIALS:
2 pieces of wool blanket, 30 x 40 cm (11$^{1}/_{2}$ x 15$^{1}/_{2}$ ins).
2 pieces of cotton lining, 30 x 50 cm (11$^{1}/_{2}$ x 19$^{1}/_{2}$ ins).
1.8 metres (71 ins) of cord.
60 cm (23$^{1}/_{2}$ ins) of satin binding.
Appleton's Crewel Wools—754 (pink), 752 (pale pink), 932 (purple),
602 (pale purple), 692 (yellow), 154 (green), 641 (pale green).

PROCEDURE:
1.   Transfer the Hot Water Bottle Cover design (page 48) onto one of the blanket pieces. Refer to 'Transferring Designs' on page 12.
2.   Embroider the design following the key on page 48.
3.   With right sides facing in, machine stitch the blanket pieces together, working two sides and the bottom.
4.   Turn the bag right side out and lightly press the seams.
5.   Stitch the linings in the same manner.
6.   Leaving the lining bag wrong side out, place it inside the wool bag.
7.   Turn an edge on the end of the satin binding and with right sides facing, sew the binding around the top of the lining bag. Turn in a second edge and cut off any excess binding. The turned edges of the binding will form a hole through which the cord can be passed through.
8.   Press the binding flat and fold the lining over so that it overlaps the top of the wool bag. Machine stitch the bottom edge of the binding to the wool bag and place another row of stitching around the top of the binding, forming a casing for the cord.
9.   Snip a small hole in the binding on the side seam that has no opening and work a buttonhole stitch around the hole.
10. Cut the cord in two and thread one piece in on one side taking it around the bag and out the same hole. Tie a knot at the end of the cord.
11. Repeat the procedure again threading the other piece of cord through the hole on the other side.

FINISH:
1.   For a neat finish, slip stitch around the bag in the middle of the seams and around the bottom of the satin binding using the Appleton's 754 (pink).

Satin Stitch
Flower

App 932, 602, 692

Satin Stitch
Leaves

App 154, 641

Bullion Rose

App 754, 752

Bows

App 752

Slippers (actual size)

Hot Water Bottle Cover
(actual size)

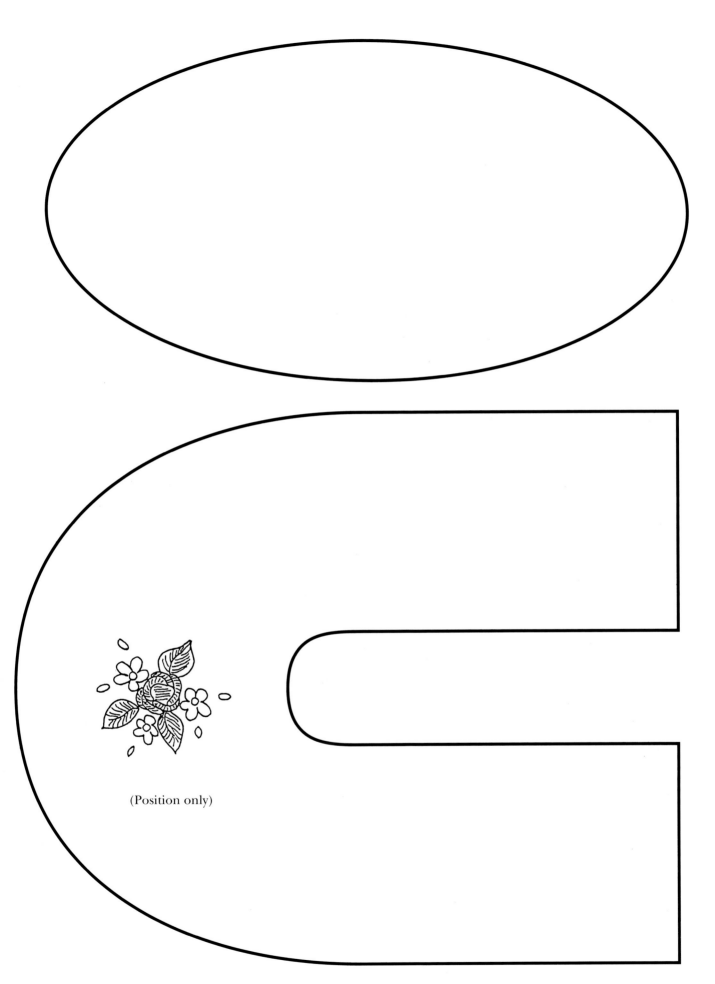

(Position only)

Lady's Bathrobe Gift Set

Pamper yourself with a touch of Victorian charm by transforming an inexpensive bathrobe into an elegant garment. Embroider roses in soft pink wools, gather cotton lace around the collar and pocket trims. As a final touch of luxury, tie a soft satin bow around the waist then coordinate it with a set of bath towels and accessories embroidered to match.

White Robe

An embroidered robe makes a delightful gift for a special friend.

MATERIALS:
Purchased robe (white).
2 metres (2¹/₄ yds) of wide white satin ribbon.
100% cotton lace (white)—measure the robe to determine the required amount.
Appleton's Crewel Wools—753 (pink), 754 (pink), 755 (pink), 641 (green).

PROCEDURE:
1.   For transferring the design onto the robe refer to 'Transferring Designs' on page 12.
2.   Embroider the collar and pockets on both sides of the robe.
3.   Slip stitch the lace onto the robe gathering slightly as you sew. Commence at the bottom of the robe on the side that wraps over and slip stitch all the way around, stopping the lace just below the waistline.
4.   Slip stitch the lace onto the edge of the pockets.
5.   Using the Appleton's 753 (pink) wool, stem stitch around the robe including the hem, pockets and sleeves.
6.   Remove the robe belt and replace with white satin ribbon.

Stem Stitch		App 753
Colonial Knots		App 753
Lazy Daisy Leaves		App 641
Rose Bud and Leaves		App 753, 754, 755, 641
Half Rose		App 753, 754
Full Rose		App 753, 754, 755

Head Band (actual size)

Hand Towel
(actual size)

Pocket
(actual size)

Dressing Gown Collar
(actual size)

Flannel (actual size)

Towel (reduced size)

53

Bath Towel, Hand Towel, Flannel and Make-up Headband

Bath Towel, Hand Towel, Flannel

The Bath Towel, Hand Towel and Flannel completes the set.

MATERIALS:
White bath towel, hand towel and flannel.
100% cotton lace (amount required determined by the dimensions of the three articles).
Lace beading (as above).
White satin ribbon (as above).
Appleton's Crewel Wools—753 (pink), 754 (pink), 755 (pink), 641 (green).

PROCEDURE:
1.   For transferring the design on these projects, refer to 'Transferring Designs' on page 12. To obtain an embroidery design of actual size for the bath towel, enlarge the design (page 53) using the 141% setting.
2.   Embroider the designs onto the towel, hand towel and flannel following the key on page 52.
3.   Measure the required amount of lace for your towel and hand towel, allowing enough for slight gathering and turning in of the edge.
4.   Measure the lace beading and ribbon and cut to required lengths.
5.   Turn under a small edge on the lace and stitch into place. Slip stitch the lace, gathering it slightly as you attach it to the bottom of the towels.
6.   Slip stitch one side of the lace beading, placing it on top of the lace edge.
7.   Thread the ribbon through the beading and anchor it in place by slip stitching the other side of the beading.

Make-up Head Band

The tie belt from the robe has been used to construct this Make-up Head Band.

MATERIALS:
Waist belt from the robe.
1.5 metres (59 ins) of white satin binding.
Velcro.
Appleton's Crewel Wools—753 (pink), 754 (pink), 755 (pink), 641 (green).

PROCEDURE:
1.   For transferring the design (page 53) onto the head band, refer to 'Transferring Designs' on page 12.
2.   Unpick the towelling belt and iron flat.
3.   Cut two pieces of towelling, 61 x 7.5 cm (24 x 3 ins), slightly curving both ends.
4.   Embroider the design onto one of the towelling pieces following the key on page 52.
5.   With wrong sides facing each other, tack the two pieces together. Tack the satin binding to the towelling, embroidered side up and sew in place with the sewing machine.
6.   Fold the binding to the back of the head band and slip stitch in place.
7.   Sew small pieces of Velcro onto each end of the band to fasten.

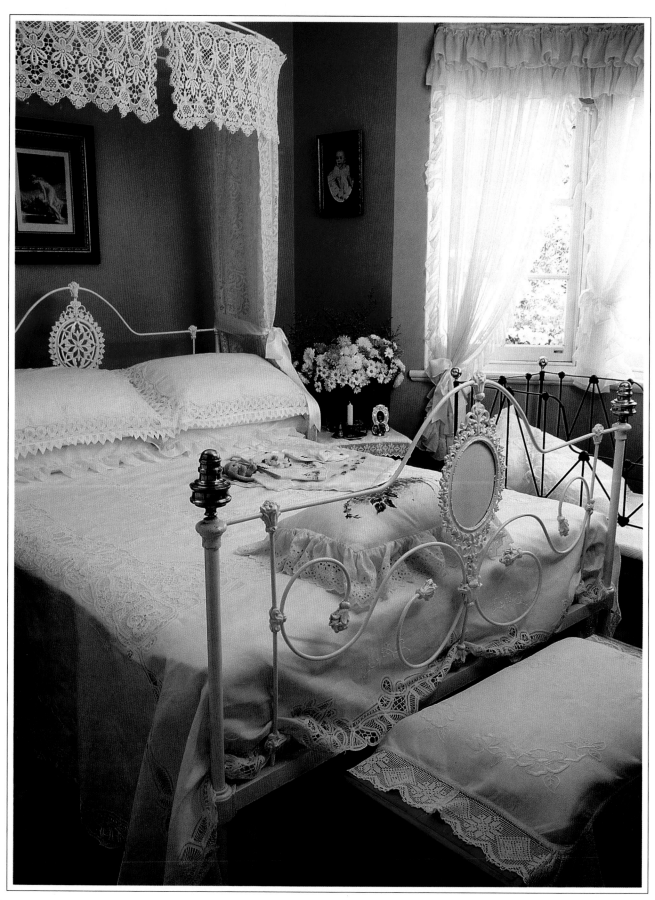

Gift Ideas

There is nothing like a handmade gift to show that special person how much you care. With a little imagination and flair you can create the most charming gifts by using touches of lace, ribbons, muslin and organdie. Gather rose petals, other flowers, spices and herbs to make fragrant pot pourri sachets just as your grandmother did. Cover tiny boxes with pretty embroidered lids. Pin cushions are easy and fun to make. Mix a variety of trims to add a creative touch all of your own. Recycle old doilies by adding your own delicate embroidery. Remember a handmade gift is truly a gift from the heart.

Pot Pourri Bag

Pot pourri bags are delightful gifts. A pretty bag can be constructed in a few hours using small scraps of fine fabrics, such as muslin, cheesecloth, organdie, ribbons and lace.

MATERIALS:
2 pieces of muslin fabric, 15 x 20 cm (6 x 8 ins).
60 cm (24 ins) of ribbon.
Small piece of lace for trim.
Small circle of soft iron-on interfacing.
Pot pourri.
DMC Stranded Cotton—3041 (purple).
DMC Broder Medicis—8223 (dark pink), 8224 (pink), 8405 (green).

PROCEDURE:
1.　On the piece of muslin fabric, mark a spot in the centre of the fabric approximately 6 cm (2$^1/_2$ ins) from the bottom of the rectangle.
2.　Iron the small circle of interfacing over the marked spot on the back of the fabric. The interfacing will provide a firm base on which to embroider the design.
3.　Transfer the design (below) onto the muslin. Refer to 'Transferring Designs' on page 12.
4.　Embroider a centre rose, surrounding it with six more roses.
5.　Work six sprays of lavender in satin stitch spaced evenly around the roses.
6.　Hand or machine stitch the seams of the bag and slip stitch the lace trim to the top of the bag.
7.　Partly fill the bag with pot pourri and tie with a generous bow.

Lavender and Leaves		DMC Medicis 8405 DMC Stranded Cotton 3041
Rose		DMC Medicis 8223, 8224

Pot Pourri Bag (actual size)

Pin Cushions

Pin cushions are fun to create and are great gift ideas. They require only small amounts of materials and make ideal introductory projects for the novice embroiderer. Here are three ideas to inspire you.

Pink Heart Pin Cushion

MATERIALS:

Small piece of pink blanketing.
90 cm (35$^1/_2$ ins) of cotton lace.
Polyester filling.
1 steel wool pad.
Tracing paper.
Pins.
1 metre (39 ins) of pink silk ribbon.
50 cm (20 ins) of green silk ribbon.
DMC Broder Medicis—8223 (dark pink), 8224 (pink), 8405 (green).
Marlitt Thread—895 (green).
DMC Stranded Cotton—523 (green).

PROCEDURE:

1.   Transfer the design (page 62) onto the piece of blanket. Refer to 'Transferring Designs' on page 12.
2.   Embroider the design.
3.   Cut a template of tracing paper using the heart pattern. Pin the template onto the embroidered blanket piece making sure the pattern is centralized within the heart and cut out the shape.
4.   Cut out a second heart shaped piece of blanket.
5.   Tack the two heart shapes together with the embroidered side facing inwards.
6.   Machine or hand sew the seams of the cushion leaving an opening of approximately 6 cm (2.5 ins).
7.   Turn the cushion inside out and press lightly around the seams of the heart.
8.   Pack the cushion with polyester filling and place the pad of steel wool into the centre of the heart (the steel wool pad will keep the pins and needles sharp).
9.   Slip stitch the opening.
10.   Slip stitch the lace into the seam around the heart gathering it slightly as you stitch.
11.   Stem stitch around the lace using the Marlitt 895 (green).

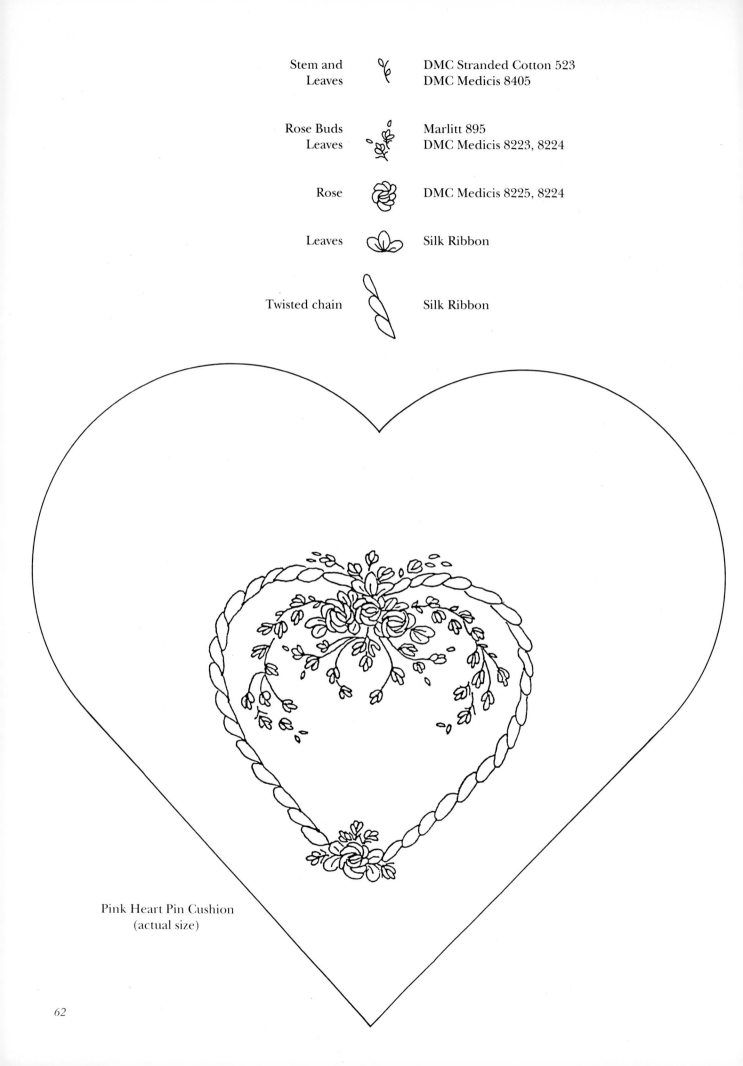

Stem and Leaves		DMC Stranded Cotton 523 DMC Medicis 8405
Rose Buds Leaves		Marlitt 895 DMC Medicis 8223, 8224
Rose		DMC Medicis 8225, 8224
Leaves		Silk Ribbon
Twisted chain		Silk Ribbon

Pink Heart Pin Cushion
(actual size)

Blue Pin Cushion

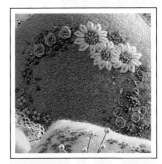

MATERIALS:
Small piece of blue blanketing.
90 cm of cotton lace.
Polyester filling.
1 steel wool pad.
Tracing paper.
Pins.
DMC Tapestry Wool—blanc.
Appleton's Crewel Wools—351 and 352 (green), 741 (blue), 692 (yellow).
DMC Broder Medicis—8223 (dark pink), 8224 (pink), 8225 (pale pink), 8221 (pale blue), 8328 (pale lemon), 8503 (tan).
Marlitt Thread—1077 (yellow), 895 (green), 1059 (blue).
Dewhurst Gold Thread—2144D.

PROCEDURE:
1. Transfer the Blue Pin Cushion design (page 65) onto the piece of blanket. Refer to 'Transferring Designs' on page 12.
2. Embroider the design.
3. Cut a template of tracing paper using the circle pattern.
4. Pin the template onto the embroidered blanket piece so that it is centred over the garland and cut out the circle.
5. Cut a second circle of blanket.
6. Tack the two circles of blanket together with the embroidered side facing inwards.
7. Machine or hand stitch the seams of the cushion leaving an opening of approximately 6 cm (2.5 ins).
8. Turn the cushion inside out and press lightly around the seams of the circle.
9. Pack the cushion with polyester filling and place the pad of steel wool into the centre of the garland. (The steel wool pad will keep the pins and needles sharp.)
10. Slip stitch the opening.
11. Slip stitch the lace into the seam around the cushion gathering it slightly as you stitch.
12. Thread a size 18 Tapestry needle with Medicis 8224 (pink), Appleton's 351 (green) and Dewhurst gold thread together in the same needle. Stem stitch around the edge of the lace.

Fly Stitch
Leaves App 352

Colonial Knot
Forget-Me-Not App 741, 692
Marlitt 1077

Hollyhock DMC Medicis 8221
Marlitt 1059

Satin Stitch
Flower DMC Medicis 8328,
8503
App 351

Colonial Knot
Leaves DMC Medicis 8224
Marlitt 895

Rose Buds DMC Medicis 8223,
8224

Rose and
Leaves DMC Medicis 8223,
8224, 8225
App 351

Lazy Daisy
Colonial Knot
Centre DMC Tapestry Wool
blanc
App 692

Blue Pin Cushion (actual size)

Fly Stitch
Leaves App 351

Satin Stitch
Forget-Me-Not  App 741, 886, 692

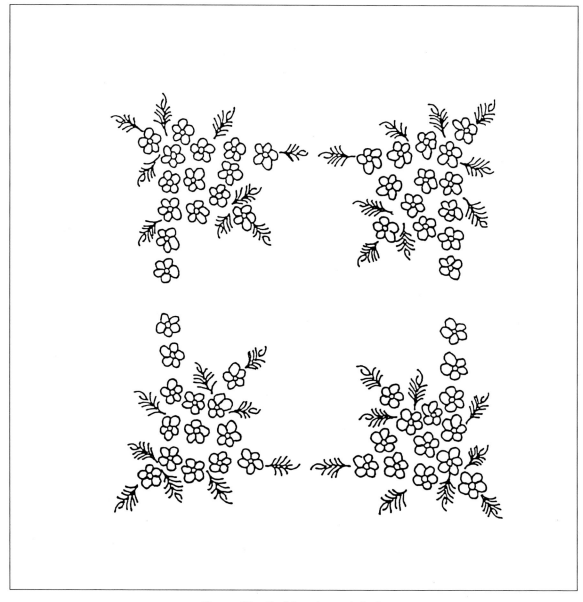

Cream Pin Cushion (actual size)

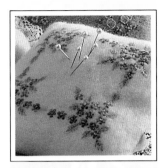

Cream Pin Cushion

MATERIALS:
Small piece of cream blanketing.
Polyester filling.
1 steel wool pad.
Tracing paper.
Pins.
Appleton's Crewel Wools—351 (green), 741 (blue), 886 (blue), 692 (yellow).

PROCEDURE:
1. Transfer the Cream Pin Cushion design (page 66), onto the piece of blanket. Refer to 'Transferring Designs' on page 12.
2. Embroider the design.
3. Cut a template of tracing paper using the square pattern.
4. Pin the template onto the embroidered blanket piece making sure that the pattern is centralized within the square and cut out the square.
5. Cut a second square of blanket.
6. Tack the two squares of blanket together with the embroidered side facing inwards.
7. Machine or hand sew the seams of the cushion leaving an opening of approximately 6 cm (2.5 ins).
8. Turn the cushion inside out and press lightly around the seams of the square.
9. Pack the cushion with polyester filling and place the pad of steel wool into the centre of the square.
10. Slip stitch the opening.
11. Using the Appleton's 741 (blue), stem stitch around the seam of the square.

Embroidered Coathanger

Fly Stitch Leaves		DMC Medicis 7871, 8405 Marlitt 895
Colonial Knot Forget-Me-Not		DMC Medicis 8211, 8314 Marlitt 1077
Violets		DMC Medicis 7896, 8314 Marlitt 1077
Bullion Stitch Daisy		DMC Medicis 8328, 8503

Colonial Knot Flower		DMC Medicis 8896, 8397
Hollyhocks		DMC Medicis 8113 Marlitt 1019, 895
Rose Tree		DMC Medicis 8132, 8818, 8426

Remember when exquisite doilies graced every room in Grandmother's house? One has been used to effectively decorate a coathanger.

MATERIALS:

Coathanger, size of your choice.

Old, or purchased, plain doily with lace edging.

90 cm (35 ins) of 10 mm ($^1/_2$ in) wide ribbon.

1 metre (39 ins) of silk ribbon (optional).

Polyester wadding.

Piece of dressmaker's tracing paper.

DMC Broder Medicis—8405 (green), 8871 (green), 8426 (green), 8818 (pink), 8113 (pink), 8132 (pink), 8211 (blue), 8328 (yellow), 8314 (yellow), 8896 (purple), 8397 (purple), 8503 (fawn), white.

Marlitt Thread—1019 (pink), 895 (green), 1077 (yellow).

PROCEDURE:

1. Fold the doily in half and mark the centre spot in which to insert the hook of the hanger.

2. Snip a tiny hole in the centre spot and buttonhole stitch around it using the white Medicis.

3. Centre the cottage garden design (below) onto the bottom edge of the doily and trace the design using the dressmaker's tracing paper.

4. Using the key as a guide, embroider the design.

5. Cut the wadding the same size and shape as the white fabric on the doily and tack into place on the back of the doily.

6. Place the doily over the hanger and screw the hanger hook back into place.

7. Making sure that the doily is folded exactly in half, hand sew it together.

8. Wind the 10 mm ($^1/_2$ in) white ribbon around the hook of the coathanger and tie a bow at the base of the hook.

9. Stem stitch around the edge of the doily using the Marlitt thread 1019 (pink).

10. If your doily has eyelet holes in the lace, thread silk ribbon around the doily and tie in the front with a small bow.

Embroidered Coathanger (actual size)

Covered Basket

Embroidered roses and a simple spot print have been used to transform a small cane basket into a charming box with a pin cushion lid, in which to keep your threads or your jewellery.

Covering The Lid

MATERIALS:
Small cane (hexagonal) basket.
Small piece of blanketing.
Braid.
Polyester filling.
1 steel wool pad.
Pins.
DMC Tapestry Wools—7123, 7122 and 7191 (apricots), 7376 (green), 7390 (green).
Appleton's Crewel Wools—708 (apricot).

PROCEDURE:
1.   Transfer the design (page 72) to the blanket. For more information refer to 'Transferring Designs' on page 12.
2.   Embroider the rose design onto the blanket piece.
3.   Trace the shape of the top of the basket onto a sheet of paper. Pin the shape to the blanket piece and cut it out allowing 1 cm ($^1/_2$ in) overlap.
4.   Fold the overlap under and press with the iron.
5.   Hand stitch the blanket shape to the lid of the basket leaving a gap in which to insert the polyester filling and steel wool.
6.   Place the steel wool on top of the polyester filling as the steel wool will keep the pins and needles sharp.
7.   When the basket has been padded, hand stitch the opening.
8.   Hand stitch the braid around the top of the blanket and the basket edge.
9.   Work a stem stitch with the Appleton's 708 (apricot) wool around the edge of the top braid.

Lining The Basket

MATERIALS:
20 cm (8 ins) of fabric.
Thick white pasteboard.
Polyester wadding.
Craft glue.
Braid.

PROCEDURE:
1.   Turn the basket upside down and trace the hexagon shape onto the pasteboard. Cut the hexagon shape to fit the bottom of the basket allowing for the wadding and the fabric.

2. Cut a piece of wadding the same size and shape as the pasteboard and glue together.

3. Cut a piece of fabric the shape of the hexagon allowing a 3 cm ($^1/_8$ in) overlap. Fold the fabric over the pasteboard hexagon and glue down the overlapping fabric.

4. To line the inside, measure around the top of the basket. Then measure the depth leaving enough fabric to sit underneath the padded base and to turn under a top edge.

5. Cut out the required fabric, sew a side seam and position the lining into place.

6. Glue the fabric base to the bottom of the basket. Turn over the top edge of the lining and glue into place.

7. For a professional look, glue or stitch braid around the top of the lining edge.

Leaves		DMC 7390
Fly Stitch Leaves		DMC 7376
Rosebud		DMC 7123, 7122, 7191, 7390
Bullion Rose		DMC 7123, 7122 7191

Covered Basket (actual size)

Embroidered Cushion Cover (reduced size)

Embroidered Cushion Cover

Embroider an elegant cushion for your lounge room or family area. A dark contrasting background highlights bunches of rose buds and forget-me-nots tied together with pretty pink bows.

MATERIALS:
Black purchased cushion cover.
1 white sheet of dressmaker's tracing paper.
Embroidery hoop.
Appleton's Crewel Wools—886 (blue), 692 (yellow), 292 (green), 641 (green), 341 (green), 142 (pink), 751 (pink).
DMC Broder Medicis—8119 (pink).

PROCEDURE:
1.   Iron the cushion cover flat.
2.   To enlarge the embroidery design (page 73) to actual size, use a photocopier set on 141%. Transfer the design onto the cushion using the dressmaker's tracing paper.
3.   Embroider the flowers, leaves and bows in satin stitch using the key as a colour guide.

Leaves		App 641
Rose Buds and Leaves		App 142, 751 App 292
Leaves		App 341, 292
Rose Leaves		App 341, 292
Leaves		App 292
Forget-Me-Nots Colonial Knot centres		App 886, 692 App 692
Bow		DMC Medicis 8119

Ring of Roses Cushion Cover

Delicate embroidery can transform a plain cream cushion into an elegant decoration.

MATERIALS:
Plain cream cushion cover.
Coloured sheet of dressmaker's tracing paper.
DMC Stranded Cottons—3042 (purple), 223, 224, 225 (pinks), 523 (green).
Appleton's Crewel Wools—692 (yellow), 351, 352, 641 (greens).
DMC Broder Medicis—8119, 8223, 8224, 8225 (pinks), 8503 (soft brown), ecru.
Marlitt Thread 1207, 1213 (pinks), 895 (green), 1077 (mustard), 1036 (cream).

PROCEDURE:
1. Transfer the embroidery design (page 79) onto the cushion using dressmaker's tracing paper.
2. Embroider the design using the key (page 78) as a guide.
3. Work the bow in satin stitch using one strand of Marlitt. Sew a fine stem stitch, also of a single strand, around the satin stitch for a finished effect.
4. To complete, stem stitch around the edge of the cushion and frill, with a single thread of Marlitt.

Pistol Stitch Flower DMC Stranded Cotton 3042

Reverse Buttonhole Stitch
Flower DMC Medicis 8224
Marlitt 1207

Bullion Daisy DMC Medicis 8223
Marlitt 1077

Forget-Me-Nots DMC Medicis 8211
App 692

Bullion Rose DMC Stranded Cotton 223, 224, 225

Rose Buds DMC Stranded Cotton 223, 224, 523

Colonial Knot
Wild Rose DMC Medicis 8225
Marlitt 1213, 895

Daisy DMC Medicis 8503, Ecru
Marlitt 1036

Fly Stitch Leaves App 351, 342

Pin Wheel Rose DMC Medicis 8119
App 342
Marlitt 1207

Colonial Knot
Wild Rose DMC Medicis 8225
Marlitt 1213, 895

Ring of Roses
Leaves DMC Stranded Cotton 223, 224, 225
App 641

Bow  Marlitt 1036

Ring of Roses (actual size)

Bullion Bunny Baby's Set

Once upon a time, there were four little bullion bunnies, all making mischief amongst the hollyhocks and daisies of an English country garden.
Embroider the Bullion Bunny designs, inspired by storybook characters to create truly memorable gifts for a special baby.

Baby's Rug

A soft, warm rug is important in a new baby's life and a treasured keepsake.

MATERIALS:
Pure wool blanket piece, (cream)—length and width 60 cm (24 ins).
2.7 metres (3 yds) of satin blanket binding (cream).
2.7 metres (3 yds) of cotton lace—width 15 mm ($^5/_8$ in).
DMC Tapestry Wools—white, 7215, 7192 and 7191 (apricots), 7390 (light green), 7392 (green).
Appleton's Crewel Wools—764 (light brown), 876 (light blue), 741 and 886 (blues), 692 (yellow), 352 (light green), 188 (cream).

PROCEDURE:
1.   To enlarge the embroidery design (page 83) to actual size, use a photocopier set on 141%.
2.   For transferring the design to the blanket, refer to 'Transferring Designs' on page 12.
3.   The DMC Tapestry Wool used in this project has been split in two, to achieve a finer texture. Make sure that the strands used are no longer than 30 cm (12 ins) because the wool tends to disintegrate.

FINISH:
1.   The satin binding, lace and stem stitch finish used on this blanket is the same as used with 'Amy's Cot Blanket'. Refer to page 23 for further information.

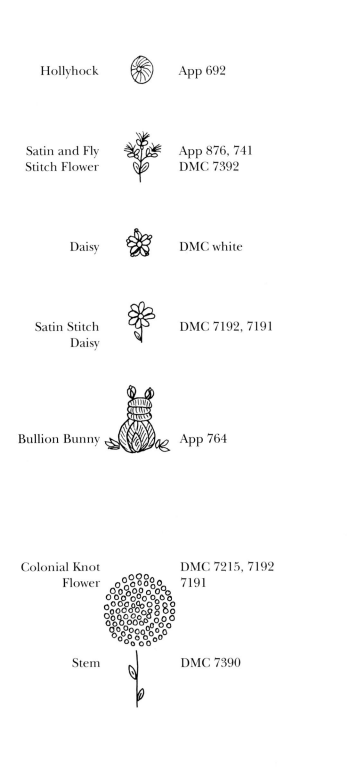

Hollyhock   App 692

Satin and Fly
Stitch Flower   App 876, 741
    DMC 7392

Daisy   DMC white

Satin Stitch
Daisy   DMC 7192, 7191

Bullion Bunny   App 764

Colonial Knot   DMC 7215, 7192
Flower   7191

Stem   DMC 7390

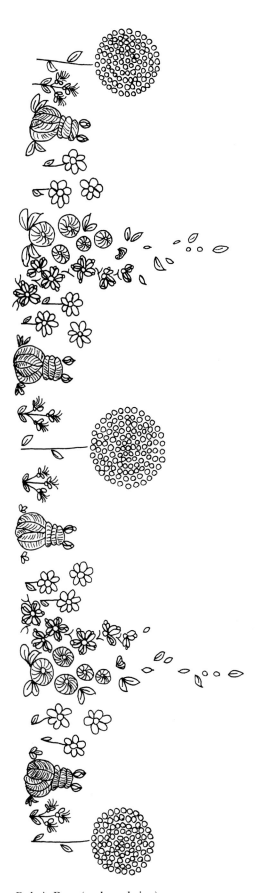

Baby's Rug (reduced size)

Baby's Cardigan

Use your skill to freehand embroider the bullion bunnies on the front of a knitted cardigan.

MATERIALS:
Plain white baby's cardigan, purchased or hand knitted.
DMC Broder Medicis—8420 (pale green), 8412 (dark green), 8119 (pink), 8211 (pale blue), 8327 (light yellow), 8313 (dark yellow), 8223 (dark pink), 8225 (light pink), white.
Appleton's Crewel Wools—764 (brown), 741 (blue), 886 (blue).

PROCEDURE:
1.   Unfortunately it is not possible to transfer a design onto a garment of this type. Use the embroidery design (page 85) in conjunction with the key as a guide to freehand embroidery of the cardigan.

FINISH:
1.   Work a stem stitch around the bands of the jumper using Appleton's 886 (blue) wool.

Baby's Bib

Add a touch of class to an inexpensive bib by removing the cotton binding around the bib and replacing it with satin. To conceal the back of the embroidery , back the bib with a small piece of cotton fabric.

MATERIALS:
Purchased baby's bib.
Satin binding (the amount required is determined by the size and design of the bib).
Small piece of fabric for backing.
Appleton's Crewel Wools—764 (brown), 341 (green).
DMC Broder Medicis—white, 8221 (blue), 8224 (pink), 8304 (yellow).
Chacopy paper.

PROCEDURE:
1.   Transfer the embroidery design (page 87) onto the bib using chacopy paper.
2.   When the embroidery is completed remove the cotton binding off the bib. Use the total length of the cotton binding as a guide to how much satin binding you will require.
3.   Cut the backing for the bib out of the piece of fabric and tack it to the bib.
4.   Tack the satin binding and sew into place by machine, sewing the backing piece of fabric at the same time.

FINISH:
1.   Stem stitch around the edge of the binding using Appleton's 886 (blue) wool.

Baby's Cardigan

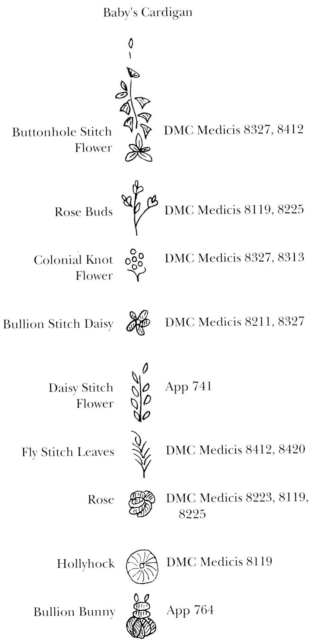

Buttonhole Stitch Flower — DMC Medicis 8327, 8412

Rose Buds — DMC Medicis 8119, 8225

Colonial Knot Flower — DMC Medicis 8327, 8313

Bullion Stitch Daisy — DMC Medicis 8211, 8327

Daisy Stitch Flower — App 741

Fly Stitch Leaves — DMC Medicis 8412, 8420

Rose — DMC Medicis 8223, 8119, 8225

Hollyhock — DMC Medicis 8119

Bullion Bunny — App 764

Baby's Singlet

Try to purchase a singlet with eyelet holes for threading ribbon through for a delicate finish.

MATERIALS:
Purchased baby singlet (preferably with eyelet holes around the sleeves and neck).
2 metres (2^1/$_4$ yds) of white ribbon—width 3 mm (^{1}/$_8$ in).
60 cm (24 ins) of cotton lace—width 15 mm (^{5}/$_8$ in).
Appleton's Crewel Wools—764 (brown), 341 (green), 886 (blue).
DMC Broder Medicis—8221 (blue), 8224 (pink), 8314 (yellow), white.
dressmaker's tracing paper.

PROCEDURE:
1.   Transfer the embroidery design (page 87) using the dressmaker's tracing paper.
2.   Embroider the singlet.

FINISH:
1.   Slip stitch the lace onto the edge around the sleeves of the singlet.
2.   If you have purchased a singlet with eyelet holes, thread the ribbon through.
3.   Thread the leftover ribbon through the eyelet holes of the neck and tie a bow in front of the singlet.
4.   Stem stitch around the sleeve, neck and the bottom band of the singlet using Appleton's 886 (blue) wool.

Baby's Booties

Add character to plain booties with embroidered bullion bunnies.

MATERIALS:
Pair of booties.
Appleton's Crewel Wools—764 (brown), 341 (green).
DMC Broder Medicis—white, 8221 (blue), 8224 (pink), 8314 (yellow).

PROCEDURE:
1.   Like the cardigan, it is not possible to transfer the design onto the booties. Use the design (page 87) as a guide for freehand embroidery.

Baby's Singlet and Bib

Baby's Booties

Colonial Knot
Flower

DMC Medicis 8119

Colonial Knot
Flower

DMC Medicis 8211, 8327

Bullion Bunny

App 764

Garment Design

Creative people are constantly seeking new ways to exercise and extend their skills. Garment design, therefore, can provide you with the exciting challenge of transforming a plain knitted garment into a boutique original.

Take a scene normally confined to a painter's canvas and create your own secret garden. Embroider sprays of flowers over a classic cable stitch jumper to suggest the essence of spring. Add a touch of sparkle to the centre of your flowers by experimenting with sequins, tiny beads and metallic threads.

Try threading your size 18 tapestry needle with wool, silk ribbon, metallic thread, or anything that takes your fancy and embroider a cardigan with decorative squiggles using the twisted chain stitch shown on page 103 in the Glossary of Stitches.

Pink Cardigan and Booties

The baby's pink cardigan has been worked on one side only to show the effect that can be achieved by adding embroidery. Using fine Broder Medicis wool, stem stitch has been worked through the centre of the rib around the sleeves, up the centre rib and around the neckline. Tiny roses have been embroidered on the sleeves, the centre band and in the centre of the buttons. The buttons have been sewn onto the garment with a cotton thread which has then been used as a base on which to embroider the tiny wool roses. Two green colonial knots have been placed at each end of the rose to form the leaves.

White Cable Knit Jumper

Even a cable knit jumper can be personalised with sprays of forget-me-nots and roses.

MATERIALS:
Hand knitted or purchased cable knit jumper.
Appleton's Crewel Wools—351 (green), 342 (green), 692 (yellow),
876 (blue), 751 (pink), 753 (pink).

PROCEDURE:
1. Embroider the flower sprays onto the jumper in the position of your choice.
2. Using the Appleton's 751 (pink), stem stitch through the centre of the cable.

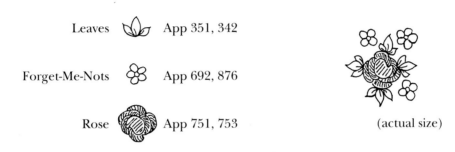

Leaves — App 351, 342

Forget-Me-Nots — App 692, 876

Rose — App 751, 753

(actual size)

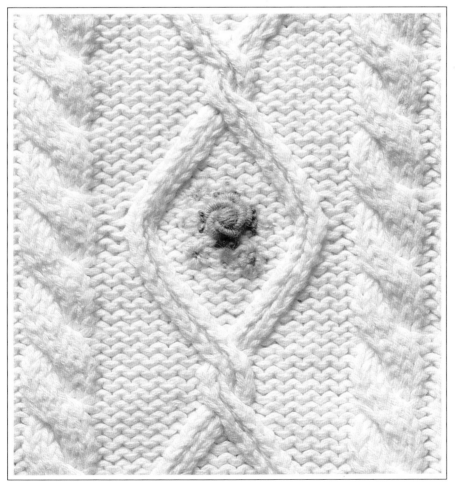

Cottage Garden Jumper

Create your own cottage garden then add to it any time the mood takes you.

MATERIALS:
Hand knitted or purchased jumper.
DMC Perlé Cotton No. 5—blanc, 221, 223, 224, 225 (pinks), 955, 396 (greens), 932, 931 (blues), 758, 754 (apricots), 676 (yellow).
DMC Stranded Cotton—420, 434, 839 (browns), 3041, 3042 (purples), 3052 (green).

PROCEDURE:
As it is impossible to transfer a design onto a jumper, use the key and the colour illustration below as a guide to create your garden.

Trellis		DMC Stranded Cotton 420, 434, 839
Wisteria Colonial Knots		DMC Stranded Cotton 3041, 3042, 3052
Fly Stitch Leaves		DMC Perlé 955, 396
Colonial Knot Flower		DMC Perlé 676, 932, 758, 754, blanc DMC Stranded Cotton 3041, 3042
Reverse Buttonhole Stitch Flower		DMC Perlé 223
Daisy		DMC Perlé 758, 931, blanc
Bullion Stitch Daisy		DMC Stranded Cotton 3041 DMC Perlé 224, 758, 754
Daisy		DMC Perlé 676, blanc
Pekinese Daisy		DMC Perlé 221, 224, 225
Pinwheel Rose		DMC Perlé 225

Roses		DMC Perlé 221, 223, 225
Roses		DMC Perlé 758, 754
Hollyhocks		DMC Perlé 676

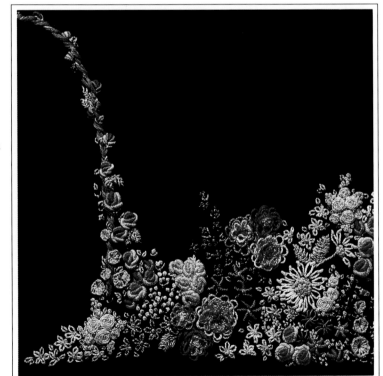

Topiary Tree Design

This delightful design would be suitable for an adult's or child's jumper or windcheater.

MATERIALS:

DMC Tapestry Wools—7223, 7221, 7200 (pinks).
Appleton's Crewel Wools—741 (blue), 692 (yellow), 641 (light green),
351 (dark green), 352 (green), 881 (cream), 764, 767 (browns).
Marlitt Thread—1077 (yellow), 1036 (cream), 1019 (pink).

PROCEDURE:

1. Transfer the design (page 95) to your garment. Refer to 'Transferring Designs' on page 12.
2. Begin to embroider using the key on page 94 as a guide.

Colonial Knot Forget-Me-Nots		App 741, 692 Marlitt 1077
Leaves		App 641, 352
Colonial Knots		DMC 7223, 7221, 7200 Marlitt 1019
Double Daisy		App 881 Marlitt 1036
Flower Stem		App 764, 767
Basket		App 764, 767
Fly Stitch Leaves		App 355
Rose Buds		DMC 7221, 7200
Half Rose		DMC 7223, 7221
Full Rose		DMC 7223, 7221, 7200
Bow		DMC 7200

Topiary Tree (actual size)

Glossary of Stitches

The stitch section of an embroidery book is the most important part. Without the practical key of stitches you would not be able to create fine works. Once you have mastered a few simple stitches you have opened the door to a whole new world of creativity.

All embroidery stitches have many uses and adaptations; experiment with them to produce fantasy flowers; your own interpretations that are produced by experimenting with the endless variety of stitches and stitch placements that are now available to you. The choice of threads also plays an influential part in how you form the flowers by the sensitive blending of threads of varying textures and colours, e.g., heavy and fine wools, perlé cottons, silks, gold and silver threads; all used to emulate nature's image of light and shadow.

Spend time playing with the stitches and threads and you will be well rewarded. There are no right or wrong ways to embroider, only different ways and you can search out your own path to beautiful work.

Every stitch that has been used in the projects in the book are included in the Glossary of Stitches.

For left-handed embroiderers, the stitch instructions should be reversed.

STARTING AND FINISHING THREADS

The back of your embroidery should be nearly as neat as the front. For most forms of embroidery you do not use a knot. However, when working with wool, you should use a knot as most of the articles are embroidered unbacked and you need them to last; they can become heirlooms handed on in time.

The knot can be completely concealed beneath the embroidery and, if worked correctly, has no tail and sits on the very end of the thread.

KNOTTING THE THREAD

1. Thread the needle. Hold the needle near the eye with the thumb and finger of the right hand.
2. With your left hand place the very tip of the tail end of the thread onto the needle and hold in place with the thumb and finger of the right hand.
3. With your left hand twist the thread around the needle four or five times.
4. Pinch the twists with your thumb and finger of your left hand and with your right hand pull the needle and thread through the twists all the way to the bottom of the thread. You will then have one perfect knot right at the end of your thread with which to commence your stitches.
5. On completing each flower, leaf, etc., return the thread to the back of your work. Conceal the knot by inserting the needle and thread through the middle of the knot and tuck it underneath the worked stitches.
6. Weave the needle and thread in and out of the stitches a few times, then anchor off.

EMBROIDERY STITCHES
BACK STITCH

1. Bring the thread through the fabric and take a small stitch backwards.
2. Bring the needle through again a little in front of the first stitch and take another stitch, inserting the needle at the point where it first came through.
3. Try to keep the stitches all the same length.

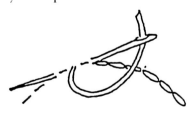

BULLION STITCH

1. Pick up a back stitch the size of the bullion stitch required. Bring the needlepoint out where it first emerged but do not pull the needle through.
2. Twist the thread as many times as is required to equal the space of the back stitch.
3. Hold the coils with your thumb and finger and ease the thread through. Insert the needle back to your starting point to anchor the bullion knot.

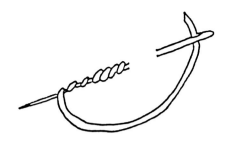

BULLION BUNNY—STEP BY STEP

Step 1
1. To form the bunny's body, bring your thread up through the fabric and take a back stitch 1.5 cm ($^5/_8$ in) in length.
2. Work a bullion stitch consisting of fifteen twists.
3. Work three more bullions of the same size placing them alongside of each other.
4. By placing your needlepoint towards the centre point when anchoring the bullions, you will make your bunny plump instead of square (diagram 1).

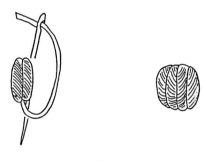

Diagram 1

Step 2
1. To work the bunny's head, bring the thread through the fabric at the top right corner of the body and take a back stitch the width of the bunny's body (diagram 2).
2. Work a bullion stitch consisting of ten twists and return the needlepoint to just slightly above where it first emerged.
3. Take a second back stitch the same size as the first and repeat the procedure again (diagram 3).

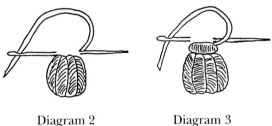

Diagram 2   Diagram 3

Step 3
1. To form the bunny's ears, bring the thread through the fabric at the left hand side of the bunny's head. Insert the needle again where the thread first came through and bring it up again 5 mm ($^1/_4$ in) from the head.
2. Loop the thread around the needle and pull the thread through. Anchor it at the top with a small stitch (diagram 4).
3. Bring the needle up to the right hand side of the head and repeat the procedure again.

Diagram 4

Step 4

1. To work the bunny's tail, bring the thread through the fabric at the bottom of the bunny into the centre of the four bullions.
2. Take a small back stitch and work a bullion stitch consisting of six twists (diagram 5).
3. Return your thread to the back of your work and finish off.

Diagram 5

BULLION ROSE—STEP BY STEP

Step 1

1. The bullion rose is best worked in three toning colours.
2. Thread the needle with the deepest shade thread.
3. Bring the thread through the fabric and take a back stitch of 1.5 cm ($^5/_8$ in) in length (diagram 1).
4. Leaving the needle in the fabric, hold the needle between your thumb and finger of your left hand.
5. Place your thumb under the needle and your finger on the top of the back stitch. This movement will hold the needle and your work firmly in place.
6. With your right hand, twist the thread clockwise around the needle fifteen times (diagram 2).

Diagram 1   Diagram 2

7. Pinch the bullion between your thumb and finger and ease the needle through the twists. Pull all of the thread through and lie it down.
8. Pull the thread again making sure the thread is nice and firm. This step is most important to prevent the bullions from becoming loose and floppy.
9. Secure the bullion by going down through the fabric returning the needlepoint back to where it first emerged (diagram 3).
10. Pull the thread through and anchor it firmly in place (diagram 4).

Diagram 3   Diagram 4

11. Work two more bullions side by side in the same manner (diagrams 5 and 6).

Diagram 5   Diagram 6

Step 2

1. Thread the needle with the next toning colour.
2. Bring the needle through the fabric to the midpoint of the three centre bullions.
3. Take a back stitch the same size as the original, placing it in the middle of the side of the three centre bullions, returning the needlepoint to where it first emerged and work a bullion of fifteen twists (diagram 7).

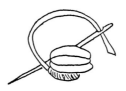

Diagram 7

4. Pull the thread through and anchor it firmly in place by again returning the needlepoint back to the midpoint where it first emerged and bring the needle and thread through the fabric.
5. Take a second back stitch the same size as the first, only this time placing it on the other side of the three centre bullions and repeat the procedure again (diagrams 8 and 9).

Diagram 8   Diagram 9

6. Turn the rose around and bring the needle through the fabric to the midpoint at the other end of the three centre bullions (diagram 10).
7. Repeat the procedure again working both sides of the centre bullions, this time slightly overlapping the last two bullions worked (diagram 11).

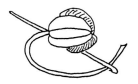

Diagram 10

Diagram 11

BULLION ROSE BUD

Step 1

1. The rosebud is worked in three toning colours.
2. Thread the needle with the deepest shade thread.
3. Bring the thread through the fabric and take a back stitch 1 cm ($^1/_2$ in) in length.
4. Work a bullion stitch consisting of ten twists (daigram 1).

Diagram 1

Step 3

1. Thread the needle with the lightest shade thread.
2. Take a back stitch the same size as the original and place it so that it lies along the side of the two overlapping bullions (diagram 12).
3. Work the bullion, this time twisting the thread around the needle twenty times. Anchor off by bringing the needle out into the fabric half a stitch length (diagram 13).

Step 2

1. Thread the needle with the next toning colour.
2. Bring the needle up through the fabric just below the bottom of the first bullion stitch.
3. Work another bullion stitch also consisting of ten twists placing it to one side of the first bullion stitch.
4. Take another back stitch on the other side and repeat the procedure (diagram 2).

Diagram 2

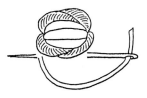

Diagram 12

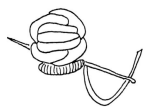

Diagram 13

4. Take a back stitch by placing the needle down through the fabric half way along the last bullion worked returning the needlepoint back to where it first emerged (diagram 14).

Step 3

1. Thread the needle with the lightest shade thread.
2. Bring the thread through the fabric just below the bottom of the next two bullions and repeat the second procedure again (diagram 3).

Diagram 3

Diagram 14

Step 4

1. Thread the needle with a green coloured thread.
2. Work a fly stitch around the bud (diagram 4).
3. Bring the needle through the fabric at the centre of the fly stitch and place a small stitch back to the starting point of the first bullion.
4. Bring the thread through to the back of the fabric and anchor off.
* The bullion rose bud can be varied by working a satin stitch centre instead of the first bullion stitch. (See *Step 1*, above.)

5. Continue working around the rose in this manner until the rose is complete (diagrams 15 and 16).
6. The number of bullions worked around your rose will vary, usually seven or eight.

Diagram 15

Diagram 16

The bullion rose can be varied by working a satin stitch centre instead of the bullion centre. This method has been used on the white dressing gown and towel set featured in the project section.

Diagram 4

BULLION TIPPED DAISY

1. Work a centre of small colonial knots (diagram 1).
2. Commence the daisy petals working from the inside to the outer edge.
3. Bring the needle and thread through the fabric at the base of the petal. Insert the needle back to where it first emerged and bring it up again just inside the tip of the petal (diagram 2).

4. Loop the thread around the needle and pull the thread through (diagram 3).
5. Take a small back stitch and return the needlepoint back just inside the petal tip (diagram 4).
6. Leaving the needle in the fabric, work 4 or 5 bullion twists around the needle (diagram 5).
7. Pinch the twists with your thumb and finger of your left hand and ease the thread through (diagram 6).
8. Pull the twists firm and anchor off by inserting the needle back to the centre base from which to work your next petal (diagram 7).
9. For an interesting effect, alternate the size of the petals (diagram 8).

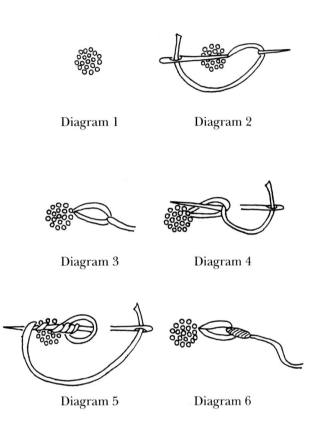

Diagram 1   Diagram 2

Diagram 3   Diagram 4

Diagram 5   Diagram 6

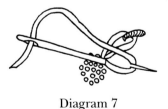

Diagram 7

Diagram 8

BUTTONHOLE STITCH

Buttonhole stitch can be worked in two ways. Try both methods to decide on the most suitable.

Method 1
1. Bring the thread out on the lower (inner) line. Insert the needle on the upper (outer) line (diagram 1), taking a straight downward stitch with the thread below the needle.
2. Pull the stitch up to form a loop and repeat the stitch working around the circle.

Diagram 1

Method 2
This method is especially good for working hollyhocks.
1. Bring the thread through the fabric at point A. Take a stitch backwards (point B) and insert the needle back slightly above where it first came through (point C, diagram 2).
2. Wrap the thread up over the needle, bring the needle through and feed backwards away from the centre to form a knot (diagrams 3 and 4).
3. Insert the needle a small space away from the knot returning it to the centre point (diagram 5).
4. Wrap the thread over the needle towards you, bring the needle through and feed backwards again away from the centre.
5. Continue in this manner until you have worked a circle (diagrams 6 and 7).
6. For a reversed buttonhole stitch, wrap the thread away from instead of towards you.

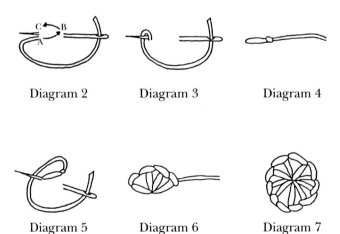

Diagram 2   Diagram 3   Diagram 4

Diagram 5   Diagram 6   Diagram 7

CHAIN STITCH

1. Bring the thread through the fabric. Hold the thread to the left with the thumb of the left hand.
2. Insert the needle where it last emerged and bring the needle point out again a short distance away.
3. Loop the thread around the needle towards you. Pull through.
4. Repeat the loop by inserting the needle point back to exactly where the thread came out in the previous loop.

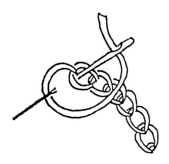

Lazy Daisy with Colonial Knot centre

COLONIAL KNOT

1. Bring the needle up through the fabric (point A). Hold the thread taut with the left hand away from the fabric.
2. Place the needle under the thread to the right and lift the thread up over the needle from left to right creating a figure eight.
3. Insert the needle into the fabric close to where it emerged and pull the working thread taut with your left hand so that a firm and tight knot is formed.

Lazy Daisy with open centre

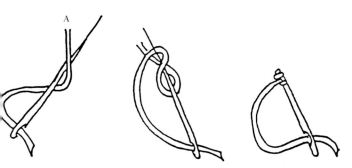

Lazy Daisy with centre of small Colonial Knots

DAISY STITCH

The diagrams which have been included show different ways to vary the daisy stitch. Exciting effects can be gained by experimenting with stitch placement, choice of threads and colour.

1. When commencing the daisy, work from the inside to the outer edge.

Tipped Lazy Daisy

Double Lazy Daisy

2. Bring the needle and thread through the fabric at the base of the petal. Insert the needle back to where it first emerged and bring it up again just inside the tip of the petal.
3. Loop the thread around the needle and pull the thread through.
4. Anchor it at the top of the petal with a small stitch.
5. Bring the needle up through the back of your work to start the next petal.

Lazy Daisy and Straight Stitch

Lazy Daisy tipped with Fly Stitch

Lazy Daisy tipped with Fly Stitch and Straight Stitch

FLY STITCH

The uses for this stitch are endless and open to your own imagination. Fly stitch is a great stitch for forming leaves and is also excellent for connecting flowers, such as forget-me-nots and rose buds.

1. Bring the needle out through the fabric to the left of where the stitch is required (point A, diagram 1).
2. Take the needle across a little to the right (point B), and take a small stitch downwards to the centre (point C). With the thread below the needle, pull the thread through and insert the needle again below the stitch at the centre and anchor in place.

FLY STITCH LEAVES

Fly stitch is the basis for the fly stitch leaf that has been used in many of the projects.

1. To form the fly stitch leaf, bring the needle up through the fabric at point A (diagram 2).
2. Insert the needlepoint at point B directly above point A and return the needlepoint back to point C, directly below point A.

3. Keeping the thread below the needle, pull it through and insert the needle again below the stitch to anchor it in place.
4. Continue working from left to right downwards to form a leaf as shown in the diagram.
5. If you want the leaf to swish to the right, place the anchor stitch to the right. If wanting it to move to the left, then anchor the stitch to the left. This technique will give the leaf its own natural movement. For wheat and lavender, place your anchor stitch straight down the centre.

HERRINGBONE STITCH

1. Working from left to right, bring the needle out on the lower line and insert it on the upper line a little to the right.
2. Take a small stitch to the left, keeping the thread below the needle.
3. Then insert the needle on the lower line a little to the right and take a small stitch to the left, this time with the thread above the needle.
4. These two movements are worked throughout. For the best result, the spaces between the stitches should be of equal size.

PEKINESE STITCH

1. Commence with a row of back stitches. Working from the left, weave through the back stitches by coming up through one stitch and down through the previous one. This stitch worked in circles and using three toning colours, starting from the outside and working inwards, makes a beautiful daisy.

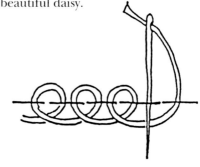

PEKINESE DAISY

This flower can be worked in many different threads, such as, Appleton's fine wool, perlé cotton, DMC wool or DMC wool integrated with metallic threads, threaded together in the same needle.

1. Work a circle of back stitches. A coin approximately 25 - 30 mm (1 - 1 $^1/4$") is a suitable size circle on which to base your flower.
2. Working from the left, bring the needle up inside the circle to the midpoint of a back stitch (point A). Come up through the next stitch and down through the previous one.
3. Continue in this way until the first circle is complete.
4. Work a second row of back stitches inside the circle and repeat the procedure.

5. Continue working the inside of the circle in this manner until you are left with a small circle in the centre of the original circle.

6. The centre of the flower can be filled in with tiny beads, sequins, colonial knots or any other way that you choose.

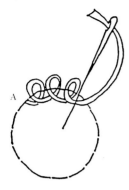

PISTOL STITCH

1. Bring the needle through the fabric at point A. Hold the thread taut with the left hand away from the fabric.

2. Place the needle under the thread to the right and lift the thread up over the needle from left to right creating a figure eight.

3. Insert the needle down through the fabric at point B.

4. To form a flower, insert the needle back to point A and repeat the procedure.

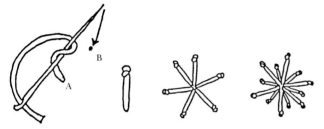

SATIN STITCH

1. Work the stitches so that they fit closely together. Care must be taken to keep a smooth and straight outside edge. The stitches may be worked straight or slanted. This may look easy, but it takes practice to make it perfect.

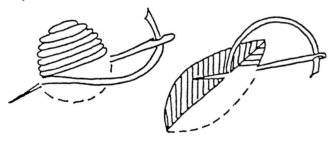

SHEAF FILLING STITCH

1. Work a group of three straight stitches side by side.

2. Then work two satin stitches over the centre binding them together.

SPIDERWEB

The silk ribbon rose and the rose referred to as the pinwheel rose are worked using the Spiderweb stitch. Many different threads can be used, such as perlé cotton, DMC wool, Appleton's wool, Medicis and silk ribbon.

1. Commence with a fly stitch (A), then work two straight stitches, one on each side of the fly stitch tail, into the centre of the circle.

2. Beginning at the centre of the circle, weave the thread under and over the spokes until the circle is filled, taking care not to pick up any of the fabric (B).

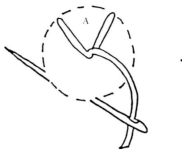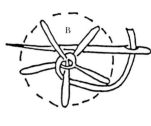

STEM STITCH

1. Work from left to right taking regular, slightly slanting stitches along the line of the design, making sure to keep the thread below the needle.

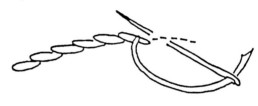

STRAIGHT STITCH

The straight stitch is a single stitch which can be worked in any direction. This stitch is especially suitable for small flower petals, small leaves and grass. It can be grouped in geometric shapes, used in lines, scattered about singly or with other stitches.

1. Bring out the needle at one end and take it down again at the other end.

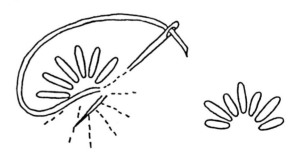

TWISTED CHAIN STITCH

This stitch is excellent for creating decorative squiggles and curves onto jumpers and windcheaters.

1. Commence as for ordinary chain stitch, but instead of inserting the needle into the place from where it emerged, insert it into the middle of the side of the last loop, taking a good size slanting stitch coming out on the line of the design. Pull the thread through.

2. Because of the movement in the wool blanket, it pays to take a much longer stitch out onto the stitch line than you would normally use when sewing, for example, a cotton fabric.

3. The loops of this stitch will need to be pulled firm, but not tight, to achieve the correct effect.

4. For braid-like effects, thread the size 18 tapestry needle with several different threads, for example, wool, silk ribbon, gold or silver thread.

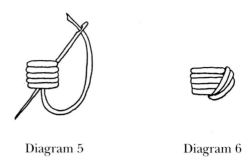

WOOL ROSE—STEP BY STEP

This rose is best worked in DMC Tapestry Wool using two or three toning colours of your choice.

Step 1

1. Using the darkest colour wool, commence by working five satin stitches approximately 5 mm ($^1/_4$ in) wide from left to right (diagram 1).

2. Keep the thread above the needle, work downwards and ensure that the tension is firm but not tight. These first five stitches will form the padding for the centre of the rose (diagram 2).

Diagram 1   Diagram 2

Step 2

1. Work a second row of stitches directly over the top of the original five packing stitches. This time, however, you will need to come out 5 mm ($^1/_4$ in) to the right hand side of your packing stitches and work upwards, from right to left, with the wool below the needle (diagram 3). You should have now finished a square with a length of approximately 1 cm ($^1/_2$ in) (diagram 4).

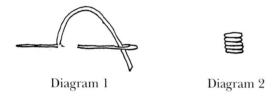

Diagram 3   Diagram 4

Step 3

1. Before commencing this step, change to the next lighter toning colour.

2. Bring the needle up at the midpoint of the base of the padding. Take the stitch to the upper right hand corner of the square, placing it with your thumb so that it lies over the top of the padding (diagram 5).

3. Bring the needle back to the midpoint of the base and repeat the stitch, this time placing it slightly below and parallel to the first stitch.

4. Return again to the midpoint of the padding and place a third parallel stitch below the second, but this time, leave the needle behind your work (diagram 6).

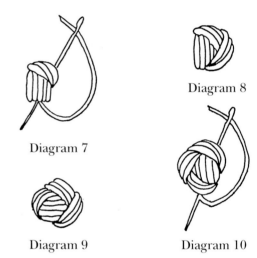

Diagram 5   Diagram 6

Step 4

1. Rotate the rose 90 degrees in an anti-clockwise direction. Bring the needle up through the fabric into the midpoint of the second base (diagram 7). Repeat the process as in step 3 above (diagram 8).

2. Continue to rotate your work until all four sides of the rose have been completed (diagrams 9 and 10). At this stage the rose could be considered complete, or you may prefer to create a more bulbous flower by using the lightest toning colour and repeating steps 3 and 4.

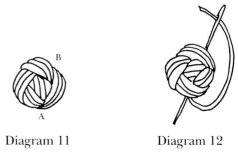

Diagram 7   Diagram 8

Diagram 9   Diagram 10

Step 5

1. To commence the third stage of the rose, find the last three stitches worked, centre to corner (A to B, diagram 11). These points are not hard to distinguish as three sides of the rose will be woven in whilst the last three stitches worked will be placed on the top of the rose.

2. Rotate the rose 90 degrees in an anti-clockwise direction. Bring the thread through the fabric at the centre (point C) and place it back through the fabric at point D (diagram 12) and repeat the procedure again.

Diagram 11   Diagram 12